With Love
Mary Boyack

Nine One One

Poems for September 11, 2001

In memory of those who died
and for those who suffer

Nine One One, *first edition,* November 2001. Printed in the United States by DMT Publishing, North Salt Lake, Utah.

ISBN 0-9713882-1-0

Acknowledgments

The poems in this book have been compiled by the Pine Nut Poets, who are members of the Utah State Poetry Society. We are grateful for the willingness of all poets in this volume to submit their work on extremely short notice, and for the decision that any profit from this book be donated to the American Red Cross.

Thanks to the students from West Elementary, Santa Clara Elementary, and Snow Canyon High School, all in southern Utah, whose artwork enhances the poems.

The many hours given by the Pine Nut Poets committee for selection, editing, formatting, etc., to bring this book to its final stage of completion, are appreciated.

Foreword

The startling events of September 11, 2001, sent shock waves across the United States and the world. As governments and authorities attempt to deal with the aftermath of the tragedy, various emotions run deep among victims, volunteers, communities, and individuals as they search to come to terms with something so unexpected and devastating.

It is hoped that the poems in this book will serve to assuage hearts, share feelings, promote understanding, and work as an effective balm to heal and comfort at a time when unity and strength are needed as much as, or more than, ever before.

Senator Orrin Hatch

Table of Contents

David Lee

Looking Down on a Small Cloudburst Across Pine Valley

Look! The sky is leaking!
—Charlie DeArmon, Post, Texas, 1949

From topland,
beaver ponds leak
across the sparkling meadow

like the sky
leaked starlight
down the valley.

Quail leak
from the oak thickets,
deer hesitate

then leak from the pines.
Trout hide beneath
leaking willowshadow

as the clouds mutter
and tremble, then leak
the afternoon rainshower.

Joan Coles

now, October

there are no words going
down on paper   no voices
or greetings   no one headed

to the water cooler   the coffee
machine   no doughnuts drawing
faces together in the break

room   no meetings   elevators
don't ply long shafts
humming   sighing   carrying

cargo from floor to floor like
coastal ships putting into port
exchanging goods for passengers

passengers for freight   there is
no thrum of wind on high
glass panels   no glitter

of glancing sun   no dreaming
into the coming Indian
summer   wires and waves

carry no messages   no words
no delight or anguish   no
love or anger   contact   sep-

aration   contracts kept or
broken   no more goodbyes
only three hundred

million
people gathering
fragments

Sue Ranglack

Wolves in Sheep's Clothing

It is one frog jump
from my window to the grass verge
that sops up damp
leavings from the long edge

of the pond. The high grass
holds secrets of fox and
shivers to itself as snakes pass
through its tangles. A bland

moon looks on. Under the sweet
breath of night there is a scent
of cattails trampled beneath the brown feet
of mud and marsh, that sour haunt

of water trapped in its dark
judgment. Every fourth exhale
of wind carries the smell, sharp
as a dog's bark in the middle of a still

moment. The curtains dance and swirl
for both sweet and sour, unnamed things leap
across boundaries of their black world
to find us unguarded in our sleep.

Clarence P. Socwell

Stumps

This morning, the sun wraps a stump
sticking up near the shore of Sapphire Lake
in gold foil, glistens against deep purple
on its shadowed side, embroiders

ultramarine ripples with orange lace.
Dead stumps of trees on land or in water
are not meant to be so moving,
pulling the eye, forcing shivers up the spine,

bristling fine hairs on arms and neck.
That should be left to a full moon through pines,
the melody of mourning doves perching
on highest branches against the sky,

flamboyant stripes of mauve and cerise at sunset–
to bands of blood-red and pure white
fluttering beside a starry blue field,
to knowing that brave men charge terrorists

to bring a plane down before it is forced
against a populace, a widow saying "God
needed him on that plane"—to knowing
that firemen rush into half-demolished buildings

to die with hearts in their open hands.
This morning's sun burnishes half-submerged
stumps with gold foil against royal purple shadows;
a meadow lark sings from a broken tree.

Maxine Russell

Tuesday Terror
W.T.C.

8:48 Jetliner explodes
on North Tower wall.

Fireball flames fly—
black smoke darkens

Windows-on-the-World.
Some jump 100 stories.

9:06 AM Second suicide
plane hits South Tower.

Veils of evil strangle
a wounded city.

Stench of hate mixes
with smell of jet fuel.

No escape for thousands
of the innocent, young,

trapped and crushed,
ignited and consumed.

Twin Towers rumble,
floors collapse.
Moment of implosion:
Impact 2.5 Richter

Hell's Holy Hijackers
strike America!

Concrete, steel, glass—
combustion, chaos.

Stairways crumble, girders
twist, elevators smash.

A blast furnace of heat!
Bodies disintegrate,

vanish, evaporate—
only a pile of shoes!

Masked figures, putty-gray
move in grief & debris.

Bitter-dry taste of lye,
concrete dust.

Firefighters persevere—
roam canyons of death,

search for the missing,
the countless unknown.
From smolder of ash, ground
zero becomes sacred ground.

N. Colwell Snell

Passing the Torch

Anyone over fifty remembers exactly where he was,
remembers the open car, school book depository,
the pink suit and pillbox hat,

the swearing-in on Air Force One,
one hand on the Bible, one raised to the square,
and the widow in the pink suit
newly stained with blood.

Americans over the age of fifty
remember the manhunt,
the real death on TV,
the aftermath, the theories,
collusion, conspiracy, subterfuge.
Day after day, year after year,
decade after decade,
the framed sequence in Dallas
kept running.

Today twin towers
were razed in a heartbeat or two,
a modern nightmare to grip a new generation—
airplanes, as bombs,
rained rubble, shattered glass and crumpled steel.
Soldiers in trenches sought the living among the dead.
All this for the old guard, so they wouldn't forget,
but especially for the new generation,
those steel-trap minds,
so they could never hope to escape
the rank aftertaste of surprise.

Erin Farish
West Elementary

Martha P. Morrise

New York Fire Fighters

A sudden fireball, fierce, immense
morning surprise, rains alarm and terror
planned by the hand of stealth, bearer
of bitter tidings conspired to give offense.

Smoke-blackened stubs of steel lurch
from the unwinding of tall walls,
the tumbling of twin towers amid calls
of fright, anguished cries that perch

on ruined ramparts. In a despair
eased by hope and kinship with grief,
these brothers, linked in courage, seek no relief
from a raven chaos of debris-burdened air.

On this tumultuous Tuesday, pain
reigns as part of the proving. The plan
of the hour emblazons every man
and woman with a discordant stain

where wanton birds squawked woe
slicing through cloud roots and blue
unruffled autumn skies to strew
death and carnage on the street below.

Firemen brave the massive weight, raise
the galling tomb of a shriveled flock
in selfless labor, construct the stricken clock
of days into lofty mazes of praise.

Richard Shorten

Sun and Stars

Not the sleek warm weapon in hand
held nervously by the empty-eyed thug,
but the knife of a steely-eyed one
who claims to do God's bidding . . .
He boards a Boeing with passengers
who in their gait, their laughter
and wistful glances, are much like me
and those I know.

With his blade at the pilot's throat,
he takes the cockpit and rips the plane
down against the 110-story tower,
another in his league repeats this
against the second tower, and another
at the Pentagon.

Multitudes evaporate,
are dislodged from family, friends,
from life. In an instant, echoing back
among them, swirl thousands
of fast-torn memories, beautiful,
wonderful, mundane, even mean,
but mostly swirl there sun and stars
that were their lives.

Marilyn Carney

Aftermath

Sharp as shrapnel,
television images
pierce complacency,
only the camera's eye
undimmed by tears.

I watch hijacked jets
sunder steel and concrete,
annihilate flesh,
waking us all
from patriot dream.

Where twin towers crowned
Manhattan skyline,
a funeral pyre smolders,
in the rubble,
America's innocence
entombed with her dead.

I feel the chill
gripping a summer day,
see the wound gaping
from sea to shining sea,
girders like splintered bones,
my nation's heart exposed.

Survivors shrouded with ash,
motionless as stone,
appear as statues
in grim memorial.

Under spacious skies,
far from amber waves,
the flag drapes ruined wall,
her stars and broad stripes
tempered by dust
that does not settle.

Gary Conners

through the eyes of a child
(soft impassioned pleas).

let's go to the beach!
can we go fishing tomorrow?
put me on your shoulders!

a litany of anticipation.

all was silenced
in a moment of thunder.

dust remained
to fulfill the promise lost.

Emma Lou Thayne

Clouds

The caustic cloud of September 11th
hangs behind my eyes like hours
squirming into each other when a child is out
too late. Life is time, ticking with no hands
to delineate an hour gone or yet to be.
Out of the smoking rubble of the dead
come those I've watched die:
Barney, our next-door neighbor, 52, on his basement stairs
gargling last breaths in Mel's arms before the last rites
his frantic wife insisted came before.
Mel's balding convivial brother, 43, on a gurney
heaving putrid air, the stench of death alive for
only me beside his open mouth whose alcoholic intake
wrenched his liver impotent, all the others
gone to the hall to write his obituary
before the morning deadline.
My omnipotent father, 59, on the 7th floor below my
pneumonia oxygen tent, on the phone before that stroke:
"Sweetie, a surprise—at home a mattress to replace
the soggy second-hand for you and Mel."
Then my doctor brother,
"Father's gone." My breathing lost with his in vapor
trying to reclaim a me departed.
My needlepoint-tiny mother, 76, holding to my hand
thumb-to-thumb for hours talking to someone not me;
my leaning close to hear, saying, "Mother I know
you always wished I'd take a gentler horse;" her brown eyes
in dark circled settings open to
"No, I always loved you on the wild one" just before
a final gasp and collecting of forces to let go.
My friend, 59, red hair, pink freckled arms,
white shoulders, toes aslant,
dead dead two hours to my touch

before the medical examiner's indifferent orderlies
collecting her,
her self left to CDs breathing her music on the night.
These dead behind my eyes yank perilous
as searching rubble for a life that isn't.
Those who wait in vain become my own.

In futile, scalding tears I take us all
around the brown leaf-scattered curves
to where the arms of Mt. Air canyon
take us in, the Little Stream gurgling life,
the giant pines dropping sticky cones for
a staccato squirrel to chomp and turn to toss away
the prickles with his tiny teeth and hands quick
as my mother's needle on her treadle machine,
then leave the slim yellow core to dart and dip his nose
for sips of the stream and dash up the retaining wall of ties
to disappear into some hole that has to be his home.
In my ancient plastic-laced rocking chair
the only clouds above the granite rocks
puff white teasing inviting imploring me
to name their shapes, childness and resurrection sure
as the distant chime of the canyon clock.

Kathleen M. Campbell

Black Veins
Scarlet Cost

Skyscrapers glint gold in September's sun.
Flight 11 ascends into a sea of blue.
Sinister hands brandish box-cutters,
divert the plane's pattern.
Carefree moments dissolve
beneath shivers of hostage terror.

The jetliner slams
through steel, glass, and flesh
slicing morning calm into smithereens,
disintegrates life into drab ashes and dust,
shreds hearts, families, peace of mind.

Day in and day out, ghastly images
and choked words crowd television screens,
deluge languishing audiences.
A stunned nation grapples with anguish.

Rescuers claw through rubble,
search for signs of life, uncover few,
but lay open black veins of terrorism,
the scarlet cost of freedom.

Doris Stengel

TIME Magazine, September 2001, Special Edition

In double-page photo spread
awkward fledglings leave the nest,
drop parallel alongside
the concrete trunk
of a dying steel tree.
School children think birds
are on fire against the pillared sky.
Teachers do not correct them.

My friend Charlotte
sky-dived at age seventy-five,
said the free fall was surreal—
peaceful, a quiet floating
on air currents,
no sense of falling.

I pray it is that way for you
who counts stories of time
tumbling by. Your necktie flutters
on the page as you hang
suspended between
here and hereafter.

A pair, man and woman, dive
hand-in-hand as they flee
into summer's perfect day,
making their own decisions
until the sidewalk.

Geraldine Felt

Implosion

A plane crashes into a tall tower
in our most populous city.
Minutes later another plane blasts
into the side of the tower's twin.
Fire roils from both wounds.
We've always known it's possible
to be struck by lightning
or clobbered by tornadoes,
but this unthinkable catastrophe—

People run, scream, stumble, fall.
Firefighters and policemen
rush into tortured buildings,
ignoring their own safety,
like in R-rated videos—content violent.
Reality of it all finally registers.

Something else is wrong besides fire.
We watch, eyes wide with fear,
repelled, but glued to the images.
The towers begin to crumple.
"Implosion" a journalist yells,
his voice loud, raspy with horror.

I've always ignored the wimpy word, "implosion"
as sounding like a pithless brother to "explosion."
Explosion conjures scenes of destruction,
dynamite, bombs, flaming debris flying outward.
Until this calamity, I'd not realized

how devastating results can be when inside heat
builds, melts, until a whole structure weakens
in complete collapse, folds over itself,
as it tumbles into trackless piles of rubble.

Rodney Dueck

Transformation

When the second plane hit,
without warning, without mercy,
everyone knew.
This was no accident.

How many moments have such power,
to sear hearts and minds,
to cleave before from after,
to change a planet's path?

Kenneth Zeeman

Images of 911

Like a Salvador Dali painting
twin spires melt into memory and time.
Hate hides the sun while white ash
snows a blizzard of concrete and humanity
on New York City streets.

Munch's *The Scream* rips the bowels
of a billion world-wide witnesses
and contorts gray-white velvet masks
of New Yorkers fleeing the morning night.

Like the hope of springtime crocuses
dashing strokes of yellow
and purple against the white,
kindness and selflessness
cradle an injured woman,
carry her through snow
out of the storm.

Flowers decked in firemen's suits
carpet pyramidal steps
below back-lit gothic windows,
Monet's *Rouen Cathedral*
emerging *in Full Sunlight*.

Rosalyn Ostler

Day of Hawks

Four hawks circle the neighborhood.
It is not their usual habitat, with mice
or other small creatures; there are only
houses below them. We have just watched
TV scenes of carnage in the East—
four passenger planes, hijacked,
become weapons aimed at unsuspecting targets.
Men run from rolling clouds, ties fluttering;
women stumble through debris in high heels,
make-up masked by dust and bewilderment.
Our minds are overwhelmed
at the sight of landmark buildings
falling as precisely as if
professionals planned their demolition.
Then we realize they have.

The viciousness shocks a nation,
a world, to a halt. Then public flags lower
to half-mast, others lift on residential streets,
blood donation centers fill, millions of prayers rise.
There are no strangers.

Do practitioners of evil ever anticipate
the American response—courage in chaos,
men and women working beyond
strength and logic to find victims;
resolution and unity in simple signs,
daytime drivers turning on car lights?
Does the hawk know
anything but scurrying, from mice?

Marillyn Johnson

Fire Wall of Hate

Speak what we feel, not what we ought to say.
The weight of this sad time we must obey.
Jon Lauwers

Force of blasts presses bones into dust, body parts,
plaster and steel fall one hundred stories to cover like
a shroud those brave firemen searching for victims,
New York's second tower is brought down as fire eats
the sky, smoke turns black, then to gray dust rising
like a beautiful mushroom. Many jump. Others walk
down stairwells led by a fireman to safety.

Terrorist hatred spreads like cancer to remote caves
and hovels, to hotels of millionaires, the jealous
zealots of a *jihad*—holy war, insane fear-stoked fire
destroying everything in its path. Fanatics choose
a "glorious" suicide, small price for death of America.

Fires of loss smolder inside loved ones who walk the
streets showing pictures to everyone, "Have you
seen him?" Flags draped on buildings and a cross
of shattered steel beams stand amid the rubble
in rank stench of lower Manhattan.

> Forty-three hundred wounded. Six thousand
> missing. One hundred fifteen bodies identified.
> Three hundred fifty missing firemen. Seventy-eight
> missing police. Twenty thousand tons of debris.
> Thirty thousand body bags requested.

Memorial services and flags stretch across the nation
putting out fires of terror that strangle our hearts.
The phoenix rises from the ashes to renew life and
hope and pride in America.

Gary Christian

Promise

On a mount of rubble in the Battery,
rescue workers raise the flag
as soldiers did on Suribachi.
It was done on a makeshift pole
at Iwo Jima, on twisted metal
in New York, where madmen
hurled symbols to the ground.

Devastation sends noxious odors
skyward. Death withholds its trophies.
Tears will not undo the past
nor stay the hand that builds.

From the ruins, greater towers
shall rise like fingers reaching
from the graves on resurrection morning.
From their heights, freedom's standard
will signal to the world.

Edith Baker

Freedom Chokes

hijacked planes explode
in tall buildings
freedoms choke
on ash-grey smoke
dreams tumble
like steel girders
lives crumble
with smashing plaster
hopes shatter
like office windows
firemen feed the fire
they came to fight
scars from this burn
will need grafting
for many tomorrows

new yorkers hug strangers
drench smoking ruins
shed tears   wipe tears
bring doughnuts and coffee
sift through hot rubble
searching for life
searching for life
searching for life

bipartisan leaders
articulate justice
american flags fan
fires of hope
the dow and the nasdaq

may fall like twin towers
but this is one fire
that is not out
yet

Rosalyn Ostler

The Day No Birds Flew

Only wind moves.
No contrails, only clouds
paint the air.
Tower voices are stilled,
and silence rides the atmosphere.
Throughout the land,
hearts stagger.
For the first time
since wings were devised,
sun shines through an empty sky.

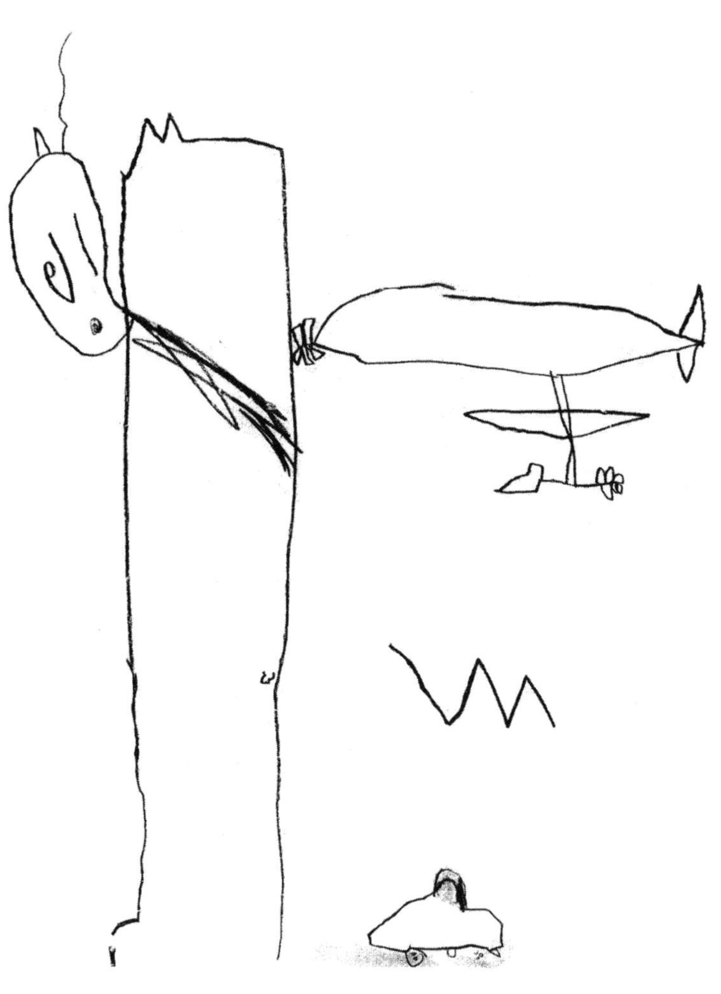

Wade Bringhurst 5
September 11, 2001

Gay Blanchard

Silhouette

New York City's proud
skyscraper silhouette
familiar against evening sunset
or misting morning light

suddenly maimed
by fierce evil's ugly force

Silent smoke rises above
crumpled steel and ashes
ashes of the dead
sackcloth and ashes of the
living left mourning
humbled turning to

God
who sends still
evening sunset
and misted morning light
on a stark strange silhouette

Gary Christian

War Begins

Darkness cloaks
the Hindu Kush,
veils dwindling waterways
and desert valleys.

A missile erupts
in charring light
from a destroyer
in the Arabian Sea,
shrieks across the night
to Quandahar.

In Kabul,
anti-aircraft artillery
stammers ponderously,
searches the sky,
brands the blackness
with searing tracks
to nowhere and to nothing.

Stealth bombers
heave their anger
on the Taliban
clustered in mountain passes
at Mazar-e-Sharif.

It has begun.
The eagle screams,
shreds with slicing talons,
tears with ripping beak.

Leslie Norris

Elegy for the Men Killed at Winter Quarters,
Scofield, Utah, 1 May 1900

When I was four years old, I watched three men
Bring my father home from the mine.
One carried him pick-a-back.
They brought him through the kitchen
And laid him soft as women could
On the bed made hurriedly in the back room.
They were in their pit dirt, lips and tongues
Scarlet in the black dust of their faces.
One of them, the biggest, said to my mother,
"I'm sorry, love, I'm afraid his back is broken."
Speaking in Welsh, which was our language then.

I make this poem for the men who sat at ease
In the safety of their evening homes; who labored
In darkness and died in the shattered earth.

George Williams was my father's boy,
His helper. He would hand my dad his pick.
When enough coal was cut, he'd slide
On his shoulders to the tight seam, scrape
The bright coal into the wide scoop
The boys used, and lift it, lump by lump,
To the waiting tram. He was fourteen.
I did not know him. I liked to think of him
At my father's side. "Tell me about George Williams,"
I used to ask. When I knew he was dead
Beneath the stone that crippled my father,
I would not be comforted. Many years ago.

I make this poem for the men and boys
Whose lives were taken wherever coal is cut,
Who went too early to the earth they worked in.

I have brought with me to Winter Quarters
Echoes of the voices of mourning women,
And the silence of the men of Gresford, in North Wales,
Where two hundred and forty lie in darkness,
And of the many dead in Senghenydd, killed
In a morning. Let the men from Finland,
The Welsh, the Scots, Englishmen, Frenchmen,
Dying far from their countries a hundred years ago,
Let them be united in the rough brotherhood
Of all the tragic mines. Let the winds blow kindly
Above them and their graves be peaceful.

I make this poem for the men who died
When darkness exploded, and for their families,
And for those of us who come after them.

LESLIE NORRIS, 12 April 2000
(Who could not write about September yet)

Karen Keith Gibson

On Their Pillow
Seen on the Larry King Show

His Tuesday responsibilities ended about
1 a.m. Wednesday. September 12th.

In quiet tones, air heavy with sorrow,
Larry extracts shards of pain from his guest.

If it hadn't been my birthday, she would have
flown out Monday, said she didn't want me
to wake up alone. She would be rushed
but it seemed worth it to both of us.
We celebrated around her packing,
my getting ready for work.

From First Class, she was ushered
to the back of the plane.
Because of her tenacity and know-how,
her collect call went through
to the Justice Department of the United States,
was forwarded to the Solicitor General.
They talked for two, three minutes.
She told them hijackers had control of the plane.

Another call, three or four minutes
this time, three or four September minutes
to last through January's chill.

The building belches black and crimson
screams that dissipate in Washington's clear air.

I wonder
if she wondered if he would find
the note she'd pinned to their pillow.

He did.

Donna K. Mackert

After the Inferno

Flames finally quenched,
ashes fallen,
smoke dissipated,
stench rises from rubble.

Steel skeletons write—
bleached-bone monuments
to man's inhumanity
to his fellowman.

Sharon Price Anderson

Collage of Grief

Thousands of silent photos
shout messages through
streets of lower Manhattan . . .
Missing: sister, father,
sweetheart, daughter.
Last seen: nine-eleven
wearing red tie, Levis,
navy skirt, diamond ring.
From posts, windows, walls,
unblinking eyes wet with
autumn rains watch heavy trucks
haul away rubble, remains.
Frozen smiles collected
at commencements,
weddings, birthdays, cry out
the nations' names.

This one is spelled the same.
Here's a haunting likeness of my
child's parent, my mother's son.
She turned twenty the day
I became fifty-one.
He was from where I was born.

The fading collage of flat
paper faces is you and me.
The ones who put them there
are we. They are all of us.

Becca Gilmore – Age 17

War

The screams of innocent people fill the air
as the giant buildings plunge to the ground
The bitter taste of death pierces the center of every soul
Angry tears flow down the cheeks of those searching
for loved ones
Their hopes are shattered as they kiss the face
of their dead
Blood-stained faces look helplessly
at the black smoke-filled sky
They reach for the light as it begins to peek through
thick dreary clouds
Praises are sung to the Most High God for a hope
of a better day
The streets are lined with red, white and blue
The skies become bright as the sun touches the lives
of those who suffer
Hope and love spread throughout the land and people
turn their lives to God
But there is still hate
Black bombs like hail plummet to the ground
shattering the lives of thousands
WAR has begun

Gary Christian

Remembrance

Disaster surgeons dismember
fallen buildings with
acetylene torches,
haul steel bones away
to places no one sees.
Death signals with stench
of crumbled skyscrapers
and putrefying flesh.

Steaming rubble marks the tomb
of thousands. It is not
a whited sepulcher. Inside
are men's bones to be borne away
to places people know.

Bereavement on its face,
America remembers, as it did
the fallen ships at Pearl Harbor.

Felice Austin

Before

After Mark Halliday

Before the sun rose in California
Before we slept late
And made love on that bright morning

Before we turned on the radio, then the television
Before the fireballs and the ash
That covered the city like a blanket covers a corpse

Before the yellow rain-slickers and orange vests
Before my poems arrived at magazines I sent them to
Before you said, "There will be fireworks this week"
And before men were burned alive in real time

Before President Bush was a tough guy
And every hand held a flag
Before you turned 27
And I crawled into bed with my yellow blanket
And cried on your shoulder, "It's the end of the world"

Before you stayed up late flipping channels
And listening to the embarrassment of rhetoric
Before the news moved in with us
        like a gabbing, unwanted relative
Before I called New York with held breath
And before the leaves, and men, and buildings fell
To be raked and bagged

Before all this…
We spoke fast and easily of the future.

Miriam Murphy

Among the Wreckage

I know why deciduous leaves change color
and the magic equivalency of the sides
of right triangles. I love words like
hypotenuse, coniferous, knight with a k,

subliminal, psyche. I applaud the daring
design of the Sydney Opera House,
the voluptuous femaleness of Georgia
O'Keeffe's flowers, the perfect timelessness

of Sophocles and Euripides.
On a summer day we rose before dawn,
filled a thermos with coffee, and wrapped
fruit and cheese. Then, seated on a grassy slope,

we watched actors emerge from the soft gray
wings of the stage in ancient Greek fashion.
We knew the vanity of Creon
or the ignorance of Oedipus meant

death and destruction. No need for oracles.
No need either to ask why we remember Attila,
Hitler, Stalin, Mao, and so many more
when their dupes and victims are nameless.

The hijackers and those who died in New York
will find anonymity. Bin Laden will not.
How well the Greeks understood vanity
and ignorance. What's more, even if the square

of the hypotenuse defines the other sides,
how little the golden leaves of autumn
explain the bombs of September 11.
So, amid this latest wreckage we, the Chorus, ask

a Sophoclean question: what is this new grief?
It is the oldest grief, offered to every generation.
Then I think of Antigone, defiant to the end,
and Creon who believed too much in himself.

Joan Coles

September 11, 2001

It isn't that the hummingbirds have gone south,
that only a sometime laggard visits the fading sage
and then moves on, or that rain brought wind, cold nights,

epiphany of flannel night clothes, but not winter bedding—
not yet, nor is it that shadows reach farther north
across the bird garden and on the burning bush, the leaves

begin to redden. It isn't that the world spins
about itself on a tilted axis, hurtles around
the sun on a long journey, shows a different face

each day. We know it well, this draining of
the golden bowl of summer, reminder that each
living thing gets only its own spiral through

the days. No more than that. It isn't that another
spring returns to find us not renewed, though we
may say so, nor that there is no new beginning,

no return to what we were, just passage through
a different place and time, until the day the world
turns to find us missing. It's only that ears awoke

to morning news, brains to catastrophe, and eyes opened
to morning sun aslant on leaves of maple, beech,
sycamore, all familiar, and yet from windows of a second-

story bedroom, everything looked different,
as if a polarizing filter, twisted,
cast, on everything, a different light.

Karen Keith Gibson

Army Ants
Eciton burchelli

They lie dormant, eager to emerge
when food supplies grow low.
Devoured deeds diminish. Voracious appetites awake.

Ants rose full-force during *Hitler's* time,
vomited contention, consumed countryside with words
and ideas opposing freedom.
Appetites satiated, they burrowed back into obscurity.
Craving food, they lived off *Korean Conflict* snacks,
emerged again, starving for *Sixties War.*
Those dreaded soldier ants, long marching columns,
followers swaggered in closed formation,
their declarations dividing countries that protected them.

Foes shrink before the ravenous demoniac insects
as they devour all allegiance along their path.
Emboldened by apathy, they infiltrate,
blend as normal ants concealed behind correctness.

After terrorists destroy landmark towers, injure
the five-sided building, create a crater in Pennsylvania,
obliterate lives, they think themselves victorious.
Armies of ants gush like geysers from underground hideouts,
spew tirades portraying villains as victims.
Eyes and ears unaccustomed to brightness,
they turn away from red, white and blue,
from blinding light of liberty,
from strains of *God Bless America,*
from heroes silhouetted against September sky.
They slink away, retreat to black holes,
cloak themselves in darkness. And wait!

Helen Keith Beaman

Eruption

Mount Hood erupts inside my heart and bleeds
its lava through my veins and out my eyes.
My mind cannot perceive such heinous deeds
that cloud the air, contaminate the skies.
The man-made storm makes buildings vomit out
their innards. Bone and flesh in towers ignite,
explode in furnace heat from Hell to tout
the lies and twisted credo of benight-
ed minds. It snows fine ash to cover all
with dusty pall and yet in irony
exposes what it hides. How it must gall
the hearts of all who prize humanity.
Where strangers stood before with vacant stares,
we kneel united in our diverse prayers.

Laurie Hornsby

Phantom Nag

The image is locked in my mind
with each waking turn in the dark
even daylight can't shake the fear
stop the tears
erase question marks

Panoramic towers
that reached to outline the sky
now lie in rubble
anguished mourning
ceaseless quandary
why   dear God   why
Vicious attack of suicide jets
commandeered by villains of war
shocked a country
scarred a nation
left heroes sobbing
on every shore
Imprisoned innocent souls
sacrificed by hate
wretched vengeance
willful malice
senseless terror
tragic fate

The image is locked in my mind
with each waking turn in the dark
I can't let it go
can't leave it alone
the pain of a savagely beaten heart

Stephanie Bringhurst

Joe Shaffer

New York, New York!
You're a Wonderful Town!

Hullo. Yep. That's my name.
You can just call me Forrest.
You ran all that way with me?
Ah'm glad you was along,
glad you's here now.
Oh, yeah. Ya know, when
Bubba was kilt in Viet Nam
and Captain Dan lost his legs,
we kinda knew who was
doin' them awful things,
and we did 'em right back.
Terrible thing they didn't
let us win that war.
Mama never told me there was
those kinda choclats in life . . .or these.
Me? I'm lookin' for Forrest, Junior.
He called me.
Said he'd be here. Waitin' for me.
Musta done looked through 165,000,000
pounds of debris. Maybe more.
Mister Laden said he wanted a Jihad,
somethin' about it bein' a holy war.
I ain't very smart, ya know,
but even I know a oxymoron.
He paid a lot to get one.
The holy war, I mean.
Well, I got me some millions,
and me and Captain Dan,

we gonna be there
on the other side.
Don't care what Uncle Sam says.
That's
all I got to say about that.

Mary Keith Boyack

Ashes, Ashes, Ashes

The screen is gray,
rapacious clouds, crumbling buildings—gray.
Even skin and eyelashes of survivors—dusted gray.
Victims interrupt monochromatic gray
showing splotches of crimson.
Still, the mood is gray,
until firemen show up in yellow.

Claire van Breemen Downes

Circle of Names

The ribbon of names runs on   runs on
looping through the whole list
known casualties   names of the dead
meaningless to them now
who have no need of naming anymore
heavy with pain for those who read
dreading to find a special name
yet every name is special
weighing upon the heart
as they cycle by
cycle by
across the bottom of the screen

they move us
more than ever-recurring images
of the plane-gone-mad
piercing the tower with flame
burying empires in toxic dust

the names circle on
having little to do with empire
the fifth-grade teacher and her class
the professor emeritus   the antique dealer
the two-year-old and her mother
the tourists just arrived in America

we are caught by names   ages   professions
hoping mother and child held each other close
that the long-married

clasped hands one more time
that the newlyweds clung tightly
relinquishing the life denied

helpless
we only sit
numbed by the circling names

Christopher Welsh, age 18

New York

There the giant stood,
Nothing could touch the behemoth.
Two metal Trojan horses crumble the unshakable towers.
Like Astyanax, the innocent plummet to their death.
Gray ash blankets the remains of monstrous hatred,
Shaking a mighty nation.
The cries of the innocent are like the children of Troy as
Mothers weep into the
Night.

Joan Weisner

The Man Who Couldn't Sleep
(A prose poem)

All night long he was thinking about something else, trying to put a name on what happened, when he looked out the window and saw a star under a first-quarter moon that appeared like an upside-down semicolon chalked on a classroom blackboard and he wondered what lesson was being taught. Of course, he knew planet Mars, the Roman god of war. Perhaps that was the message, though he had moved away from myths a long time ago. No man in the moon either, just his footprints. Now distant places are gone. Halfway around the world there's a God-wills-it zealot cloaked in a centuries-old white sheet who watches civilization dig and dig and dig through steel and bone rubble heaped upon a great city. It's still not clear to him how this will be written in history. Only God knows... but which one?

Carol Clark Otteson

An Eighty-Year-Old Father Grieves for His Son

Rod of my femur   bone of my bones
carry my broken bones with you
my feet immovable as stone
gather me into your going

Carry my broken bones with you
earth cracks and splinters in its bones
gather me into your going
the crystal is shattered   the hands move on

Earth cracks and splinters in its bones
the ground quivers and moves away
the crystal is shattered   the hands move on
the wheelchair wheels go round and round

Your voice rings out above the sound
the ground quivers and moves away
my feet immovable as stone
rod of my femur   bone of my bones

N. Colwell Snell

Afghan

She was angry with herself
slipping up like that
running out of red-orange yarn.
She had mesmerized herself
looping and looping the hooked needle,
changing the yarn over and over again.
Light blues make the sky;
gray and brown sprinkle ash
and thicken already heavy air;
yellows jump out in hard hats and slickers,
squeeze past red fire trucks, white ambulances.
Then there is black,
black smoke that billows,
hearts that ache and sizzle black
clear to the pit of the stomach.

She had all the colors:
green, purple, navy blue, tan
for shocked masses fleeing—
red, white, blue for flags at half-mast,
crimson for blood.
But red-orange for the lethal fireballs
that brought the buildings down
was gone,
and she was angry with herself,
getting caught short,
unable to finish the job.
Now she would have to wait.
Not that it mattered, really.
It was not a gift,

it was not for somebody else.
It was for her alone,
a way to vent the seething,
to convince herself that it was okay to be alive
and walk the streets again.

Star Coulbrooke

After War

We move about the day
with well-contained despair;
each photograph of terror
scatters pick-up-sticks
behind our aching eyes.

Nothing will repair
the devastation in our minds,
this picture of the future:
bodies strewn, wreckage,
no one left to bury the dead.

Maurine B. Haltiner

Phoenix Lost

Each piece of this poem lies
buried in rubble. Dust too refined
shrouds skeletons of Twin Towers
blasted open in flaming blossoms.
I have searched for a single rhyme,
a bit of phoenix to pull from multi-tons
of melted metal. But images of heavy death
wheel and whirl, a Danse Macabre
inside my head. Wordsworth, I recall,
never forgot golden daffodils, fawning
petals, thousands, millions, enough
to stop traffic on the Milky Way.
We shall recover. There will
be time for my small villan-
elle blown to hell.

Theda Bassett

Do You Hear the Drums?

Flags flutter at half-staff, fly everywhere
carry a reverberating rhythm of the drums
pulled from a *Les Miserables* scene. But
in New York City, on the debris lines, fighting
against time, these men have no thoughts of singing
"Drink with me". They seek their fallen brothers,
fight to break down the chaotic barricade
created by the enemy. With tenacity and endurance
of many Jean val Jeans, they lift steel girders,
hand buckets of rubble along, reach out
to preserve life, bring back human dignity.
As their shifts end, their eyes depict a prayer
of the desperate, "Bring him home."
That quality that ignites an electric fire in each
of us, that allows heroes to surface,
lies at the heart of America.

Kevin Clark

The Awful Gray Awful

It still looks like a picture
of Jerusalem or Beirut,
the awful gray awful rising
from its smoldering pile.
Even after a month of stench
& autumn rain, it covers all
like an acrid film,
mixing like vinegar
in the sweat of relief workers
who dig & haul, sort & find,
weep, then repeat.

It sweeps across the weeping nation
riding the dust from ground zero
breezing by a president's promises
with a glance at the Joint Chiefs' plans
then to the clouds, where bomber pilots
& fighters are up to their elbows in surgical
strikes against fanatics
bunkered in rubble of their own.

It creeps down streets lined with flags,
is churned by cars waving flags,
whistles through trees
& whips across plains
slamming screen doors across the open
heart of everyday America.
American blood unites beneath
this awful gray awful
that dusts the republic wave by wave,

day after day
reminding us of who & what we are
who our heroes are
who the villains.

This we know: an end will be given.
Rubble clears
dust settles
& perps will be left
with nothing

not even a handful of trinkets & beads.

Joyce Nuttall

Stacked Deck

Between mouthfuls
of a stacked deck of tuna on rye
he tells me his friend's mother died.
Stuffing in the last over-sized bite
he whirls off the stool and out the door.
Nothing more.
Yet the wonder in his voice told
of the pain he borrowed,
trying it on like an unfamiliar suit
in a dress rehearsal.

Carol Clark Otteson

Remembering Something Big
(Lincoln Memorial circa 1941)

His eyes look out of stone, immense,
brooding with the power of seated kings.
A child before the marble throne
wishes to climb that colossal knee,
touch the mouth of the man of sorrows,

reaching with a longing we cannot name
as if the monolithic surely saves
the unions we might wish or die for,
tells us bonds will fall away and cast
us larger than we ever hoped,

remembering a time we could believe
in mythic hovering benevolence,
could see a clear white stone as center place,
touch the huge veins smooth and permanent,
feel the fingers curled around the chair.

Bill Ruesch

Waking America

When they make the movie
the screams will siren
off the walls just under
the legal decibel threshold.
We'll cringe in our seats
cover our eyes and let
the popcorn spill.

When they make the movie
they will have forgotten
the silence:

the endless swallow,
the inhale that stays
in the chest too long,
the emptiness of denial,
the hope that it was all
a mistake, a bad dream
we can pinch away.

Todd Palmer

Angela's Response

Heavy attendance urged us on,
But any assignment was trivial.
We moved ahead anyway
To spite them.
To eyes vacant and gray,
Sick as the morning sky

I explained the lesson:
"Vary the subject-verb syntax
Using only the words given,"
The copy fuzzy from every-year use,
The exercise safe and familiar to me
Until my throat caught on sentence two:

A thick, polluted sky obscured
The buildings across the bay.
Simple enough, shift *across the bay* up front,
But the clock froze again,
No hands rose to bail us out
Until Angela gently spoke:

After the explosion, a thick polluted sky
Obscured the buildings across the bay.
And we sank in electric silence,
Swam in the boil of Angela's anger.
Then following protocol, we rose
Dutiful as the sun.

But we meant the pledge,
We felt allegiance
Perhaps for the very first time.
And justice for all?
Even the meek cut new teeth
Sharper than boxcutter knives.

Marina Santiago, 6th Grader

Bird Spirit

Flying high in the sky
the bird looks down
at the ground so far below.
The bird can fly above it all.
The bird can be a spirit,
the spirit of the freedom
that we have lost,
our spirit in the sky
with no limits.

Sue Ranglack

Ablaze in the Garden

And we bit each other
as fire bites,
leaving wounds in us
Pablo Neruda

It was there on the front page,
the computer screen,
the television every quarter-hour;
a picture of a chrysanthemum
blooming in brilliant shades
of yellow and orange
on the side of a building
where you would not expect
to find such terrible beauty.

One by one,
the postman, the musician,
the student, the grocer,
unable to resist,
plucked that flower,
tucked it in buttonholes,
pinned it to lapels,
twined it through tresses.

We all walked around
cities with eyes askance,
the pungence of that flower
sharp as fresh blood,
a pale ghost riding
just over our left shoulder,
petals still burning.

And the flame ate into us,
branded us from the inside out.
Filigrees and curlicues
in the shape of hands
appeared on our flesh
so that anyone seeing us would know
we all came
from the same garden.

Laurie Hornsby

Confession

You called from the air
knowing you'd never return
and that love
was all that mattered now

With calm repose
you spoke the words
trying to make them bigger
their simple paucity hurting as

you made certain he knew
and that he would tell the children
so they would always remember
that their mother didn't die in vain.

Helen Keith Beaman

To the Knees

thou...shalt bear a son, and shalt call his name Ishmael; because the Lord hath heard thine affliction...his hand will be against every man, and every man's hand against him.

He is my brother, vastly passionate
this child, bin Laden, who forges young his link
to God. His mother feeds him milk of faith,
his father bread of dissidence, then treads
with him the wine of discontent until
he's bloody to the knees, the hips. Confirms
him stranger, bound to no man, country, home,
or law. His baptism, a flame that will
not flicker, smolders gold until it's fanned
to red, a firebrand to kindle other
hearts that burn to cleanse the earth, to rid
our world of infidels who call the same
God by a different name, esteem Him lightly
and profane in vain, repeating, Oh my god,
my god, my god. The planes explode so hot
skyscrapers melt, innocents burn to ash.
Who can judge the dead? My brothers, sisters,
husbands, wives, all dead in the heat of hate,
blown away on winds of doctrine that forgot
to love. How many tears, how much blood,
will it take to extinguish his fire?

Lee C. Snell

I'm Sorry, I Can't Come to New York

My feet are nailed to Utah;
my outgoing flights
laden with balm for hurt hearts
and sore spirits are grounded with the others.
I would air freight a tear and an I love you
to every sufferer.

As it stands, UPS is all I can muster.
It's on its way, on its way....
picking up packages across
the nation.
I hope it helps.
Hold on until it arrives.

Maurine B. Haltiner

Mourning

Across the deserts of Afghanistan
old women, and young, drown
in the silence of sea-blue burqua
and their own tears.

Helen Keith Beaman

Yasmin

He leaves early before the birds
notice the morning. Except for his
softly chanted prayer, he is silent
so he won't wake me or the baby.
I stretch, roll over, nest my head
in his lingering scent. I get up, wipe
crumbs where he has cleaned
after his hurried breakfast, turn on
the television, mute it, watch as I
prepare Ana's bottle. I glance
at the screen, think they are razing
some old building. Alert now, I turn,
see flames, smoke burgeoning from the
World Trade Center. A plane torpedoes
into the second tower. I switch on the sound.
Johnny will already be there, his unit one
of the first at the scene. I call the unlisted
number he has given me. No answer.
He's already working to save lives. I scan
ashes, smoke, and debris, imagine I'll catch
a glimpse of him. Thirteen hours pass.
I feel like I have been strained through
the screen. I feed Ana, even play, though
I am not here. I am there, the fiery rubble
searing my soles, my eyes. No word
from his station. Reporters, desperate,
replay the horror. I'm snared in the
revolving nightmare. Heart slams
against my sternum, rebounds
in ears and throat, then freezes

in a tiny cube. It's all a dream.
I wither like a leaf onto our bed,
my edges curling in, tremble
from the tempest that has twisted me
adrift. To my left
the tube keeps playing. To my right
I see his towel crumpled on the floor.
I need to frame it, cling to the
palpable proof that he was here
this morning. I embrace his pillow,
hold on to the fading trace of him.

Shawn Dallas Stradley

Sanctuary

The sorrow of war,
the grief of violence,
turn to God for benevolence.

LaVerna Johnson

Recruiting Faith

Yesterday—September tenth,
our grandson became
a new Marine, enthused
with visions of the
man he soon would be.

Today—September eleventh,
Trade Center towers
explode innocence, crush
weight of melted ribs,
roil clouds of ash.

Tomorrow will
witness hatred,
rescued faith—
will weep for life, liberty,
          for sons, grandsons—
                    unknown tomorrows.

Gail Schimmelpfennig

The Day Stands Still

Today is a day to stop,
stand still, try to dispel
the sense of impossibility
that clings like sticky cobwebs
to images of deliberate destruction.

Today is a day to hold close,
touch with no excuses,
stroke skin of dear ones again.

Today is a day to leave work piled
on desk or shelf,
ignore your surroundings,
focus attention
on a television screen.

Today is a day to count,
to mark other days by,
before the attack
or after the attack.

Today is a day to pray for strangers,
families of strangers,
the human family,
people just like you,
this nation,
this world.

Rodney Dueck

Experiential Knowledge

America saw from afar Kosovar and Serb,
Muslim and Jew, Hutu and Tutsi,
Irish Catholic and Irish Protestant,
Pakistani Muslim and Indian Hindu.

Familiar world over,
now Americans understand
what is known in the Middle East.
Satisfaction of hatred has its price.

Islamic Fundamentalists and Americans,
entangled. What a difference
when we are involved,
when we experience carnage.

LaVerna Johnson

Undimmed By Human Tears*

We hear your song, America—
the rhythm of your seas,
fog horns encore through roar of waves,
thin flutes in mountain's breeze,
tin wails of trains throughout the night,
strains—thrums of planes above,
staccato notes of taxi cabs—
this chorus that we love.

I sing my song, America,
my small discordant tune
lost in a symphony of time
that rushes by too soon.
Though once a cherished lullaby
to calm through awesome years,
my song crescendos freedom's beat
smote on a forge of tears.

We sing our song, America,
each one throughout the land
rejoicing in the knowledge that,
united, we will stand.
Cacophony of terror struck
cannot still us, as long
as generations harmonize,
combine in freedom's song.

*Katherine Lee Bates

"Oh, that that earth which kept the world in awe,
Should patch a wall + expell the winter's flaw."

"I am become death, shatterer of the worlds."

Dan Bright

Senator Orrin Hatch

America, United

We have seen the face of evil
We have shed a nation's tears
We have felt a threat to freedom
And to all that we hold dear
Now a mighty wave is growing
As we hear our country's call
But the world still waits and wonders
Will we rise or will we fall
        As we bury fallen heroes
        Many broken hearts must heal
        But in the ruin and the rubble
        Our spirit is revealed:

          Refrain:
          America united! Working side by side
          America united! Hope still burning bright
          Those who would divide us did not realize
          From the smoke and from the ashes
          America will rise . . .United!

We have felt the force of terror
There is sorrow in the land
But through the drifting dust of chaos
Lady Liberty still stands
And the miracle of freedom
Gives a comfort to us all
For the ones who try to hurt us
Only strengthen our resolve

We are holding hands together
For we know our destiny
They have tried to find our weakness
But this is what they see:

Refrain:
America united! Working side by side
America united! Hope still burning bright
Those who would divide us did not realize
From the smoke and from the ashes
America will rise . . .United!
(Repeat refrain, modulate up, big ending)

Words and music by Orrin Hatch and Janice Kapp Perry

Gail Schimmelpfennig

New Glory

Red and white stripes,
white stars on deep blue,
American flags weave
through American minds now,
rippling through air like the notes of
"God Bless America"
or spread flat as a map of Manhattan,
bold as an airline emblem,
covered with an invisible sheen
of tears, sweat, air molecules
that still vibrate
from final cell phone calls,
radiating a glow like candles
placed before American embassies
around the world
in spontaneous shrines,
crisp and snappy like
a fast-walking New Yorker
on his way back to work.
Images of yellow-banded
firefighter coats
seem to flash between
the five points of those stars,
and some of the stripes
ooze American blood
donated at Red Cross chapters
throughout the heartland.
This old flag's got
a lot of glory left in her.

Pat Cutting

The Aftermath

Early morning synapses conjure
a conundrum, Apollo-like
          "Stitch the patches
                    . . .(blank) the swatches"
I can't read the inked scratches
I noted between waking and sleeping.

Perhaps Apollo, too, left spaces
for his priests, who strove to patch
conflicts tearing their world apart.
Baste it together, connecting
the swatches one to another to another.

We moderns, too, can at least try to stitch
our world together, word by carefully
chosen word. Not just a touch up,
a surface patch, but a full four-
dimensional trapuntal, emerging
from a two-dimensional background
of unconditional love and compassion.

A genuinely regenerated society
reunited, all the way to the depths,
person to person, linking new villages
with old, joining nation to nation,
faith to faith. A world in which
the all of us and the each of us can live
in peace and security, eagerly
          connecting person to person.

Geraldine R. Pratt

To Utah's Nicholas Taylor, Boy Scout

September 11, 2001, a Hollywood fantasy,
not real in New York City, not in the USA.
Godzilla, nowhere to be seen, had let go
the airplanes from his grip and arrowed them,
stabbed them—one, two—into World Trade Towers,
three—into the Pentagon,
four—into a Pennsylvania field.
Unbelievable, a horrible fiction, with trick
photography, manikins plunging to earth
in business clothes, twin towers blasted
to stubs in fiery rolling smoke
and noxious rubble.

Two thousand miles away, seeing but not
having heard, felt, smelled the catastrophe,
I am shielded, conditioned by that TV screen—
not real. I watch, listen, do nothing.

Nicholas, twelve, had watched his dog
Riley killed by a car two years before. On TV,
Nicholas saw rescue dogs work the ruins. He
plunged into jobs to earn money to help.

Aid poured in. Nicholas led, others supported
him onward, found ways to help through him.
The JetBlue Airlines flew him and the funds
to the vets' field hospital for the search dogs.
He visited the firemen, who, with their dogs,
continued to risk their lives.

I cannot assess the enormity of six thousand
lives, shattered, burned. And the children,
bereaved—what of them?
Some saw the face of Satan in the smoke.
Someone said nearby grass died afterward. Fire,
smoke, seem unquenchable, hang in unbreathable
air. Do the dogs have boots for their scramble
through shards of glass and metal?

Nicholas did something.
And now he hopes to get another dog.

Susan Atkin

Unfurling

A wounded flag on a windless day,
Torrents of red American pain
Bleed into the shadow's darkening stain.
A wounded flag clings steadfastly to its pole
Hangs onto faith.
And hope.
Never again will it be this low.
For when the brave blue field rises,
The rest will follow
To unfurl the stars of our indivisible soul.

Mary Keith Boyack

Keep America For Me

Hear my earnest prayer, oh Father
Hear me ask on bended knee
At this time of strife
Shed a ray of hope on life
Keep America for me

Let me see old Glory proudly fly
Unfurl its colors bright
Red for courage, blue for honor
And purity wave white

Help us comfort those who sorrow
Let each stand with dignity
Down a troubled road
Let us bear another's load
Keep America for me

From this land of hope and refuge
Help all nations to breathe free
Heal their hearts from hate
No more strangers at the gate
Keep America for me

Let me see old Glory proudly fly
Unfurl its colors bright
Red for courage, blue for honor
And for purity wave white

From Alaska to the Gulf Coast
From New York to Tennessee
States in beauty dress
With abundant harvest bless
Keep America, my homeland, for me

Till the mountains fall to ruin
Till the shores desert the sea
Till the moon turns cold
Still my heart is yours to hold
Keep America for me
Keep my homeland safe for me

Bob Eberth

close enough to hear the harps

up a staircase
of a thousand steps
i will carry you
halfway to heaven
then release you
to find blue sky
while i descend
still searching
for green grass
and sweet water

Marian Ashdown

One Nation

You are not alone in grief.
This nation suffers too.
Hands of fellowship and love
extend to each of you.

You may never be aware
how many prayers are said.
Sent heavenward to follow
those brave souls we call dead.

Death is just a word, you know.
Justice is not served
by the definition
of this cold and earthy word.

In the weeks that follow
be assured and know
our nation, on its knees with you,
will find a way to grow.

Sandy Inman

One Candle

The news of September 11th spilled from TV sets,
poured down the streets and into my classroom.
Wide-eyed seven-year-olds stood for news time,
telling of the horror, not quite sure where New York was.

I pulled down the U.S. map, reassuring them,
"Utah is a long way from the tragedy."
Then we practiced subtraction problems
and watched our caterpillar change into a chrysalis.

The grim facts continued to be shared for days.
Hoping to put closure to the children's fears,
I asked them to draw and write
about what they had seen and heard.

Walking down the rows of children, I viewed picture
after picture of airplanes crashing into buildings,
exploding fireballs, and people falling with "Help!"
ballooning from their mouths.

My heart grew heavy as I realized
the horrific images these children
would carry in their memories
forever.

Then, on the last row, a child had drawn
herself and her mother,
each holding a burning candle.
The child looked up at me and smiled.

Jane Shulman
New York, New York

Tulips and Dill

1.
I found a sprig of dill
as crisp and green as spring
alongside wilted leaves
soggy, black and rotten.

Now how that sprig survived
in the dark back of the fridge
with day after day of neglect,
I will never know.

But there it was, that sprig,
crisp and April green,
a promise of the spring
that may not come again.

2.
The yellow and violet tulips are tall and erect
standing poised to open.
The tulips in bunches
in a bucket at the florist remind me of springs gone by
and awaken hopes of springs yet to be.

Autumn this year has weighed like a sodden blanket
as the lightness of summer exploded in fire
as bodies were flung from windows and melted in steel
as the towers collapsed, floor by floor.

The weight of each floor's collapse is borne on the backs
of every New Yorker as we walk the streets
carrying on with love and work and worship
as if life still mattered as it did before.

Yet the tulips in bunches in the bucket
at the florist are singing
a different song. In the yellow and the violet
I sense the murmur of emerging life pushing
through frigid soil, aching to be born.

Sharon Price Anderson

Mourning

All night long I have been
filling my basket with
deafening images of disaster
choking, blinding smoke
crippling cries of despair
unanswered questions
grief and other burdens
too great to bear.

Needing healing, I will leave it
at the Master's feet and rise
with heart as light as morning.

Rodney Dueck

Joy of Another Kind

Warmed by our sun,
we occupy one planet,
breathe one atmosphere,
drink from one river of life.

Born from material nature,
'red in tooth and claw',
we compete, contend,
are driven by illusion,
our belief in separation.
Here the predator is king.

Blinded, win-lose spirit knows
ephemeral joy in victory,
shame in defeat.
Through the eyes of fear,
it sees what there is to see,
the need to dominate.

Born from another nature,
rooted in being,
we know, experience,
live in this present moment.

Seen through the eyes
of compassion, relationships
evoke interdependence, love,
collaboration, synergy,
openness, creativity,
joy of another kind.

Joyce Larson

September 11th

As terror fills the sky at dawn
and light is gone,
we question why
so many die.

Oh Lantern, spill thy golden rays
to turn our gaze
and light our path
away from wrath.

In prayer we turn to thee in hope
to help us cope,
and walk the path
with healing staff.

Marty Whitaker-McGill

September 11, 2001

The towers of commerce housed beings much like ourselves,
in a vertical city, an icon on a small island,
ocean- and river-bounded,
once the home of persons and animals,
living quietly under the trees.

Another lovely icon stands not far away upon her pedestal
...looking outward
welcoming our travelers and newcomers to the shore
...taking an eager step forward.
May she be perceived no other way.

The world changed in a moment found beyond belief,
though we thought ourselves inured to images of disaster
sold as entertainment on large screens and small.
Reality is not the same.
Truth cannot be given monetary value.

We suddenly are a large loving family again,
remembering better times,
while we long for now-stilled voices,
warm smiles, daily returns to homes near and far away
from the repeated scenes of carnage
visited upon us in betrayal of our trust.

The Lord surely met many of our New York brothers and sisters
partway home and has cradled them in His arms.
Think of them that way, and be comforted.
We cannot know more.

The mystery of the other side will not be solved until we take
our own trip.
Wish them well on reaching the end of their journey.
Think of the love they are feeling in their welcome there.

Mary Keith Boyack

Black Rain, Golden Harvest

Wherefore, lift up the hands which hang down,
and the feeble knees.
Hebrews 12:12

I am in the bowels of Hell;
bones and concrete grind, scrape, scream.
We swim thick black air through raining debris.
Pain hangs like drenched blankets of blood,
searing heat splatters hope, shatters resolve.

I shed my clay, slip from pain,
watch mass of ruin, mounds of grief ebb from view.
I am shot toward the Light,
find ineffable beauty, prisming perfect peace.
The gatherers are gently bringing souls,
like sheaths of cherished grain.
Those plucked too green—sent back to ripen.

A being of Light scans my heart and mind.
Contrite, I number my sins, burn to confess;
He asks only how well I have sown and reaped love.

The veil is taken from my eyes; past, present, future are one.
I see men of darkness furrow evil, seed hate, harrow carnage,
plot to ravage scores of thousands of Americans.
But hope ascends on wings of prayer,
Seraphic concourses descend, inspire altered plans, near misses,
to mortal eyes, miracles—myriads are saved.
Harvesters deliver victims to His bosom.

I awake amid rubble, havoc's roar.
Earth angels in yellow fire hats come with stretchers,
multitudes more assuage, give succor, stand ready
to lift up hands that hang down, strengthen feeble knees.
Heaven has hallowed this ground.

Lola Haskins

October, 2001

On the Withlachoochee last Saturday,
seven turtles in graduated sizes queued
on a log, routine as the osprey nests,
empty this time of year, routine as

the occasional alligator, its blunt nose
and hooded eyes half-submerged
as are most fears most of the time,
until a plane flies into a building

or a son can't be found. We
are spoiled, you and I, guilty of
saying of the good dark bread
on our plates not *how delicious,*

but *where's the rest.* And so
with the osprey nests, the turtles,
even the palms leaning so low
they parallel the water. But now

a wood stork flies over, with
its black-edged wings. And
another. And when we look left,
where river-flow complicates

into cypress creek, we see them:
hundreds of wood storks, hunched
like priests in the trees. And I
remember that morning in Cairo,

years ago, when a black-veiled
figure next to me, on the side
of the aisle that was all women,
turned, and took my western hands

in hers as if my fingers might be
breakable, as if she loved them,
and said, in the only language
we both understood: *Pass this on.*

Thad Box

When the Trade Towers Fell

I warmed at the bosom
of mother earth.
I sought strength
in beauty of her mountains.

Both we and Afghans
live in rugged wrinkles
of our mother's hide.
We are her children.

When we sow wheat
our mother feeds us.
Tears flow when we put
land mines beneath her skin.

Peter Meinke

Morrocco

Marrakech Meknes Fez Casablanca
names on a map deep in our minds
minarets & almond trees laying long shadows:
cobblestone streets under keyhole arches
shine in the darkness like broken teeth

The soul is a camel
with a hump full of sentimental images
clumping across real deserts
seeking the perfect oasis that is no mirage
(no one has ever reached it)

Marrakech Meknes Fez Casablanca
the walled cities are truly beautiful
and corrupt   In the center they decay
like molars: the pain is spreading
a white path for revolution

What shall happen to the almond trees?
They shall be burned with bazaar & babouche
their seeds shall burst underground from the heat
Green shoots will spring up
their bitter leaves nibbled by lost camels

Mikal Lofgren

First Cries

...there were only 9 million Iranians before World War II; today there are 57 million and their average age is 17. Radical Islam, with its extreme and black and white solutions, is a young person's faith.

David Talbot

I'm trying to remember
when my average age was 17.
How black seemed white and white,
black so the chess game of life
was played on a gray dimensionless field
where the rules I knew did not
apply. The gridwork gone
I made the planet mine, a place
where tree and flower, bird and beast
stood individual, unique in mind
until my world was as full of things
as Noah's ark was on the 300th day
of living in tight quarters.
My once-gray place now crowds me
out and darkness is welcome, but,
as always, I listen for the first dove at morning—
the cries that welcome each dawn.

Shawn Dallas Stradley

Forever Changed

The wind still blows across the land,
the sun still crosses the sky,
but I will remain changed,
like my grandparents were changed
in the beauty of a single morning.
Collectively, we will remain changed forever.

I honestly thought I would never see the day,
a day like today.
Perhaps I was naive.
Perhaps I was arrogant.
I believed this would never happen,
in my lifetime, here, in America.
As generations of achievement accumulated
into rubble,
it became a day without airplanes
crossing spacious skies.
America the Beautiful, abruptly awakened,
forced to slow down, to contemplate,
to mourn, evaluate and gather strength.
In the wake of disaster perspectives change.

The wind still blows across the land,
the sun still crosses the sky.

LaVerna Johnson

A Minute: Ode to Authors

Within your poems are words that reach
our hearts to teach
of things our minds
might never find.

You melt cold angst and fear's blizzards.
Oh, word wizards,
you loan us wings
good writing brings

as we explore your thoughts of hope.
You help us cope. . .
Ah, no. It's more:
You help us soar.